Teach Your Child to Read

300 Short Easy Sentences

English - Persian

Name

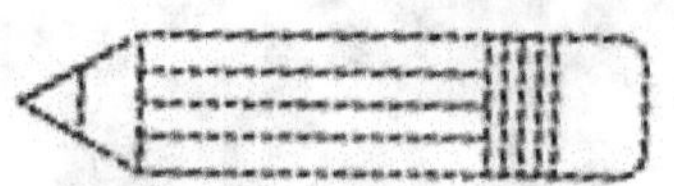

I Can...

- [ ] read the 1st sentence.
- [ ] read the 2nd sentence.
- [ ] make a sentence from a picture.
- [ ] color a picture.
- [ ] Draw a picture.

The frog is going to a party.

.قورباغه به مهمانی می رود

The happy frog is wearing a green hat.

.قورباغه خوشحال یک کلاه سبز پوشیده است

Name 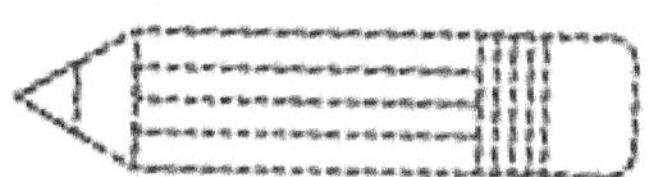

I Can...

- [ ] read the 1st sentence.
- [ ] read the 2nd sentence.
- [ ] make a sentence from a picture.
- [ ] color a picture.
- [ ] Draw a picture.

Owl likes to read big books.

جغد دوست دارد کتابهای بزرگ بخواند.

A smart owl is reading an alphabet book.

یک جغد هوشمند در حال خواندن کتاب الفبا است.

Name

I Can...

- ☐ read the 1st sentence.
- ☐ read the 2nd sentence.
- ☐ make a sentence from a picture.
- ☐ color a picture.
- ☐ Draw a picture.

Come on! The ice cream truck is here!

ابیا دیگه! کامیون بستنی اینجاست

He is driving a big icecream truck.

او در حال رانندگی یک کامیون بزرگ یخی است.

4

I Can...

- [ ] read the 1st sentence.
- [ ] read the 2nd sentence.
- [ ] make a sentence from a picture.
- [ ] color a picture.
- [ ] Draw a picture.

Dragons are very friendly and have scales on their backs.

اژدها بسیار دوستانه هستند و مقیاس هایی در پشت خود دارند.

The dragon is waving his hand.

اژدها دستش را می کشد.

Name

I Can...

- [ ] read the 1st sentence.
- [ ] read the 2nd sentence.
- [ ] make a sentence from a picture.
- [ ] color a picture.
- [ ] Draw a picture.

This ram lives in the farmhouse.

این قوچ در مزرعه زندگی می کند.

Ram has a large horn and fluffy wool.

رام یک پشم بزرگ شاخی و کرکی دارد.

Name

I Can...

- ☐ read the 1st sentence.
- ☐ read the 2nd sentence.
- ☐ make a sentence from a picture.
- ☐ color a picture.
- ☐ Draw a picture.

The bunny likes to eat carrots.

.اسم حیوان دست اموز دوست دارد هویج بخورد

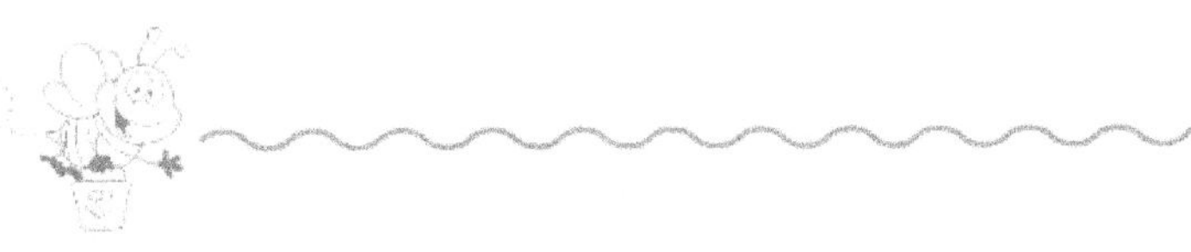

Rabbit thinks that the juicy orange carrot looks yummy.

.خرگوش فکر می کند هویج نارنجی آبدار جالب است

Name

I Can...

- [ ] read the 1st sentence.
- [ ] read the 2nd sentence.
- [ ] make a sentence from a picture.
- [ ] color a picture.
- [ ] Draw a picture.

The clown likes to give out balloons to little kids.

دلقک دوست دارد بادکنک به بچه های کوچک بدهد.

Funny, Mr. Clown is giving away colorful balloons.

خنده دار ، آقای دلقک بالن های رنگارنگ را به شما هدیه می کند.

Name

I Can...

- [ ] read the 1st sentence.
- [ ] read the 2nd sentence.
- [ ] make a sentence from a picture.
- [ ] color a picture.
- [ ] Draw a picture.

The clown is juggling balls for his performance.

دلقک برای عملکردش توپ های زوزه گرایی دارد.

Talented, Mr. Clown is juggling five red balls.

آقای دلقک با استعداد ، پنج توپ قرمز را در دست دارد.

Name

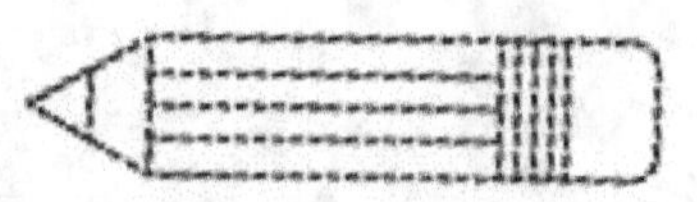

I Can...

- [ ] read the 1st sentence.
- [ ] read the 2nd sentence.
- [ ] make a sentence from a picture.
- [ ] color a picture.
- [ ] Draw a picture.

The Easter Bunny is going to give out chocolate eggs.

عید پاک اسم حیوان دست اموز قصد تخم مرغ های شکلاتی را دارد.

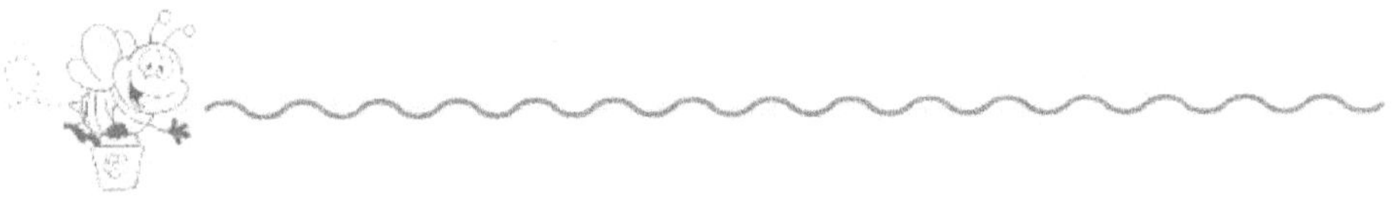

The rabbit goes out to buy more orange carrots.

خرگوش می رود تا هویج نارنجی بیشتری بخرد.

Name 

I Can...

- [ ] read the 1st sentence.
- [ ] read the 2nd sentence.
- [ ] make a sentence from a picture.
- [ ] color a picture.
- [ ] Draw a picture.

The pencil is drawing a zig-zag line.

مداد نقاشی خط زیگ-زگ است.

The Pencil is saying hello to you.

مداد به شما سلام می کند.

Name 

I Can...

- [ ] read the 1st sentence.
- [ ] read the 2nd sentence.
- [ ] make a sentence from a picture.
- [ ] color a picture.
- [ ] Draw a picture.

The pencil put on a big smile and went to work.

‏.مداد لبخند بزرگی را پوشید و به سر کار رفت

The Pencil is leaving to go on a long relaxing vacation.

‏.مداد در حال عزیمت به تعطیلات آرامش بخش طولانی است

Name

I Can...

- [ ] read the 1st sentence.
- [ ] read the 2nd sentence.
- [ ] make a sentence from a picture.
- [ ] color a picture.
- [ ] Draw a picture.

This snowman is my friend, and he is a helper of Santa.

این آدم برفی دوست من است و او یاور سانتا است.

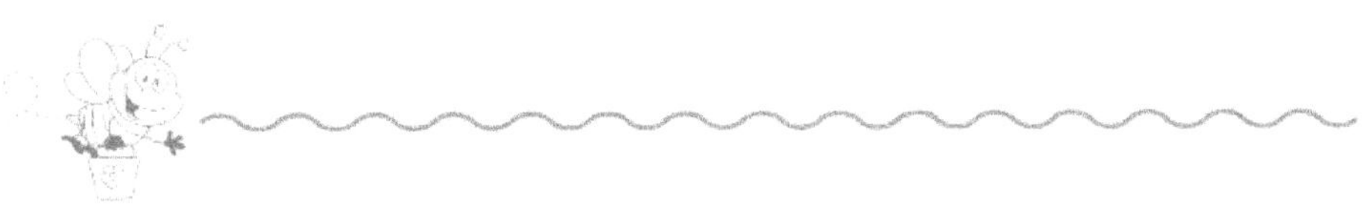

Mr. Snowman is celebrating Christmas by the decorated tree.

آقای آدم برفی با درخت تزئین شده کریسمس را جشن می گیرد.

Name

I Can...

- [ ] read the 1st sentence.
- [ ] read the 2nd sentence.
- [ ] make a sentence from a picture.
- [ ] color a picture.
- [ ] Draw a picture.

The octopus is working as a chef and serving food.

اختاپوس به عنوان سرآشپز مشغول به کار است و غذا را سرو می کند.

Chef Octopus is serving a delicious turkey dinner.

سرآشپز Octopus در حال تهیه یک شام بوقلمون خوشمزه است.

Name

I Can...

- [ ] read the 1st sentence.
- [ ] read the 2nd sentence.
- [ ] make a sentence from a picture.
- [ ] color a picture.
- [ ] Draw a picture.

Santa is happy.

.سانتا خوشحال است

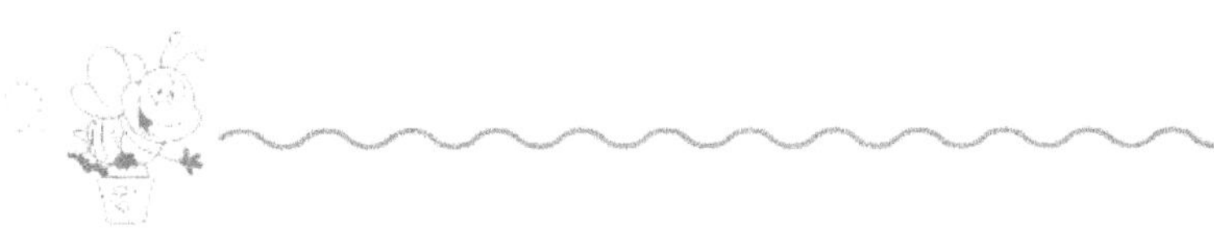

Santa Claus is giving extraordinary presents to excited kids.

.بابا نوئل به بچه های هیجان انگیز هدایای فوق العاده ای می بخشد

Name

I Can...

- [ ] read the 1st sentence.
- [ ] read the 2nd sentence.
- [ ] make a sentence from a picture.
- [ ] color a picture.
- [ ] Draw a picture.

The bear likes to eat sweets.

خرس دوست دارد شیرینی بخورد.

Teddy is licking a red and white candy cane.

تدی در حال لیسیدن آب نبات قرمز و سفید است.

Name

I Can...

- [ ] read the 1st sentence.
- [ ] read the 2nd sentence.
- [ ] make a sentence from a picture.
- [ ] color a picture.
- [ ] Draw a picture.

The book has a wand.

کتاب یک گره دارد.

The cereal box got a magician set for Christmas.

جعبه غلات یک جادوگر را برای کریسمس آماده کرد.

Name 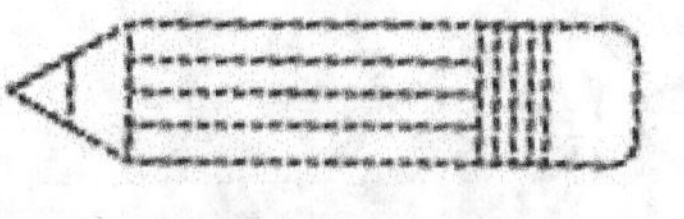

I Can...

- [ ] read the 1st sentence.
- [ ] read the 2nd sentence.
- [ ] make a sentence from a picture.
- [ ] color a picture.
- [ ] Draw a picture.

The bear has a present.

خرس هدیه ای دارد.

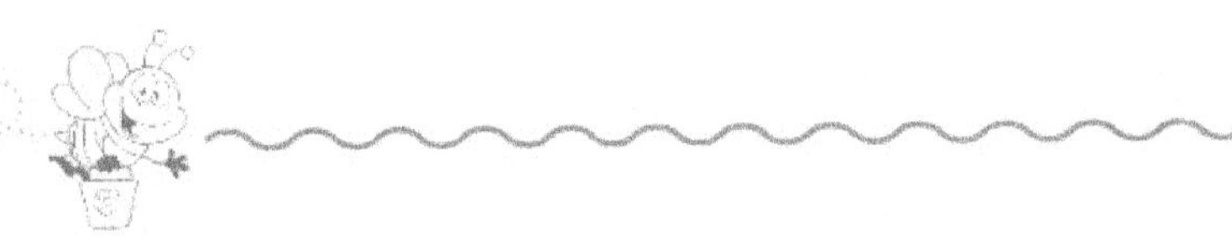

Happy Teddy is opening his box of presents from Santa.

مبارک تدی در حال باز کردن جعبه هدایای خود از سانتا است.

Name

I Can...

- [ ] read the 1st sentence.
- [ ] read the 2nd sentence.
- [ ] make a sentence from a picture.
- [ ] color a picture.
- [ ] Draw a picture.

Santa is going to give out presents.

سانتا قصد دارد هدیه دهد.

Santa is lugging a large brown bag of gifts to his sley.

سانتا در حال چمدان کردن یک کیسه قهوه ای بزرگ برای هدیه دادن به دخترش است.

Name 

I Can...

- ☐ read the 1st sentence.
- ☐ read the 2nd sentence.
- ☐ make a sentence from a picture.
- ☐ color a picture.
- ☐ Draw a picture.

I made a snowman.

آدم برفی درست کردم.

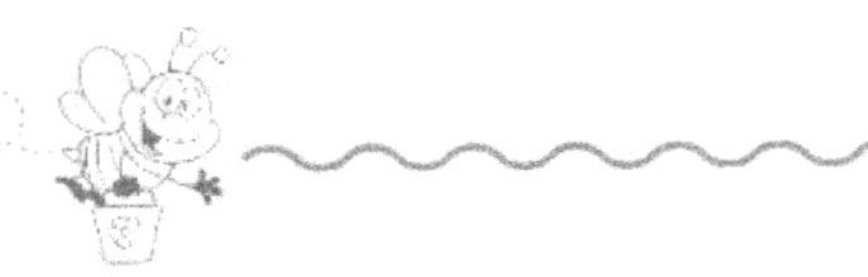

Mr. Snowman is holding a broom and saying goodbye.

آقای آدم برفی در حال برگزاری جارو و خداحافظی است.

Name

I Can...

- [ ] read the 1st sentence.
- [ ] read the 2nd sentence.
- [ ] make a sentence from a picture.
- [ ] color a picture.
- [ ] Draw a picture.

The parrot is colorful.

.طوطی رنگی است

The green parrot came from the forest to the zoo.

.طوطی سبز از جنگل به باغ وحش آمد

Name ________________

I Can...

- [ ] read the 1st sentence.
- [ ] read the 2nd sentence.
- [ ] make a sentence from a picture.
- [ ] color a picture.
- [ ] Draw a picture.

There are a lot of animals.

حیوانات زیادی وجود دارند

The animals are happy being together again.

حیوانات دوباره از کنار هم خوشحال هستند.

Name

I Can...

- [ ] read the 1st sentence.
- [ ] read the 2nd sentence.
- [ ] make a sentence from a picture.
- [ ] color a picture.
- [ ] Draw a picture.

The man is wearing a belt.

.مرد کمربند دارد

The carpenter is fixing something.

.نجار چیزی را برطرف می کند

Name

I Can...

- [ ] read the 1st sentence.
- [ ] read the 2nd sentence.
- [ ] make a sentence from a picture.
- [ ] color a picture.
- [ ] Draw a picture.

The rabbit is very young.

خرگوش بسیار جوان است.

The magician plays a trick.

جادوگر یک ترفند بازی می کند.

Name 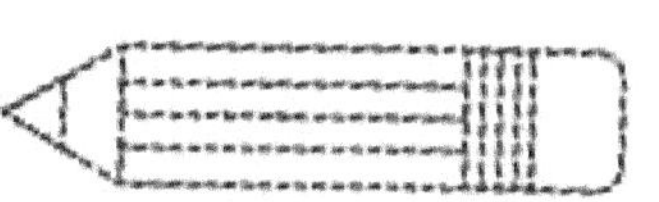

I Can...

- ☐ read the 1st sentence.
- ☐ read the 2nd sentence.
- ☐ make a sentence from a picture.
- ☐ color a picture.
- ☐ Draw a picture.

He has a potion.

او یک معجون دارد

The scientist is making a potion.

دانشمند در حال تهیه یک معجون است.

Name

I Can...

- [ ] read the 1st sentence.
- [ ] read the 2nd sentence.
- [ ] make a sentence from a picture.
- [ ] color a picture.
- [ ] Draw a picture.

He is wearing sunglasses.

او عینک آفتابی دارد.

The policeman is mad.

پلیس دیوانه است

Name

I Can...

- [ ] read the 1st sentence.
- [ ] read the 2nd sentence.
- [ ] make a sentence from a picture.
- [ ] color a picture.
- [ ] Draw a picture.

He has a bucket of paint.

‫او یک سطل رنگ دارد.‬

He likes to paint.

‫او دوست دارد نقاشی کند.‬

Name

I Can...

- ☐ read the 1st sentence.
- ☐ read the 2nd sentence.
- ☐ make a sentence from a picture.
- ☐ color a picture.
- ☐ Draw a picture.

The man has a hat.

مرد کلاه دارد.

The postman is giving out the mail in the early morning.

پستچی صبح زود نامه را ارسال می کند.

Name

I Can...

- [ ] read the 1st sentence.
- [ ] read the 2nd sentence.
- [ ] make a sentence from a picture.
- [ ] color a picture.
- [ ] Draw a picture.

He has a walkie talkie.

.او یک تالوک ویکی دارد

He is going to work with his suitcase.

.او قصد دارد با چمدان کار کند

Name

I Can...

- [ ] read the 1st sentence.
- [ ] read the 2nd sentence.
- [ ] make a sentence from a picture.
- [ ] color a picture.
- [ ] Draw a picture.

He is sleepy.

.خوابش میاد

The delivery man sent us a package.

.مرد تحویل بسته ای را برای ما ارسال کرد

Name

I Can...

- [ ] read the 1st sentence.
- [ ] read the 2nd sentence.
- [ ] make a sentence from a picture.
- [ ] color a picture.
- [ ] Draw a picture.

He is wearing a bowtie.

‫.او کمانی پوشیده است‬

The waiter is serving juice.

‫پیشخدمت در حال نوشیدن آب است‬

Name

I Can...

- [ ] read the 1st sentence.
- [ ] read the 2nd sentence.
- [ ] make a sentence from a picture.
- [ ] color a picture.
- [ ] Draw a picture.

He has a suitcase.

او یک چمدان دارد.

The engineer is holding a wrench.

مهندس در حال نگه داشتن آچار است.

Name

I Can...

- [ ] read the 1st sentence.
- [ ] read the 2nd sentence.
- [ ] make a sentence from a picture.
- [ ] color a picture.
- [ ] Draw a picture.

The chef has a napkin.

سرآشپز یک دستمال دارد.

The chef serves delicious-looking food.

سرآشپز غذاهای خوشمزه ای را سرو می کند.

Name

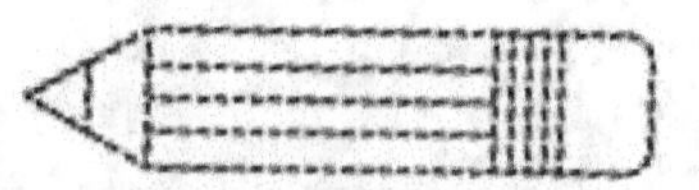

I Can...

- [ ] read the 1st sentence.
- [ ] read the 2nd sentence.
- [ ] make a sentence from a picture.
- [ ] color a picture.
- [ ] Draw a picture.

The rooster has a big beak.

.خروس منقار بزرگی دارد

The chicken is saying hello to us.

.مرغ در حال گفتن سلام ماست

Name

I Can...

- [ ] read the 1st sentence.
- [ ] read the 2nd sentence.
- [ ] make a sentence from a picture.
- [ ] color a picture.
- [ ] Draw a picture.

The bird is small.

پرنده کوچک است

The chick is on the telephone talking with his friend.

.جوجه به صورت تلفنی در حال گفتگو با دوست خود است

Name

I Can...

- [ ] read the 1st sentence.
- [ ] read the 2nd sentence.
- [ ] make a sentence from a picture.
- [ ] color a picture.
- [ ] Draw a picture.

That is my ring.

.این حلقه من است

That is a beautiful ring.

این یک حلقه زیبا است

Name

I Can...

- [ ] read the 1st sentence.
- [ ] read the 2nd sentence.
- [ ] make a sentence from a picture.
- [ ] color a picture.
- [ ] Draw a picture.

The duck has three eggs.

.اردک سه تخم دارد

The duck has a big nose.

.اردک بینی بزرگی دارد

Name

I Can...

- ☐ read the 1st sentence.
- ☐ read the 2nd sentence.
- ☐ make a sentence from a picture.
- ☐ color a picture.
- ☐ Draw a picture.

The swan is beautiful.

قو زیباست.

The graceful swan is striding through the water.

قو برازنده در حال عبور از آب است.

Name 

I Can...

- [ ] read the 1st sentence.
- [ ] read the 2nd sentence.
- [ ] make a sentence from a picture.
- [ ] color a picture.
- [ ] Draw a picture.

The girl is wearing a dress.

دختر لباس دارد.

The maid is cleaning our room.

خدمتکار مشغول تمیز کردن اتاق ما است.

Name 

I Can...

- [ ] read the 1st sentence.
- [ ] read the 2nd sentence.
- [ ] make a sentence from a picture.
- [ ] color a picture.
- [ ] Draw a picture.

The boy is running.

پسر در حال دویدن است

The little boy was running.

پسر کوچک در حال دویدن بود

Name

I Can...

- [ ] read the 1st sentence.
- [ ] read the 2nd sentence.
- [ ] make a sentence from a picture.
- [ ] color a picture.
- [ ] Draw a picture.

He is a musician.

او یک موسیقیدان است.

He is playing a lively tune on his flute.

او در حال پخش لحن پر جنب و جوش در فلوت خود است.

Name

I Can...

- [ ] read the 1st sentence.
- [ ] read the 2nd sentence.
- [ ] make a sentence from a picture.
- [ ] color a picture.
- [ ] Draw a picture.

He looks joyful.

‫او خوشحال به نظر می رسد.‬

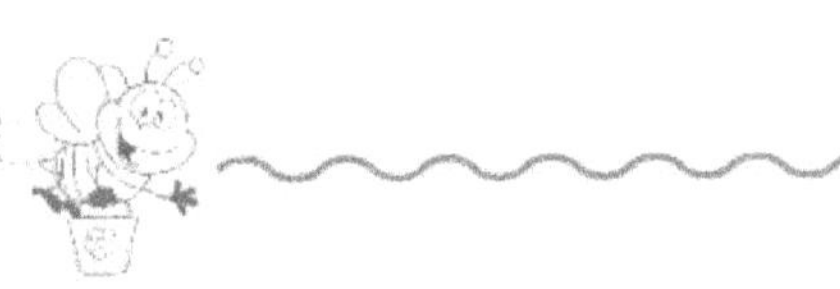

That boy works in a band and plays the drum.

‫آن پسر در یک گروه کار می کند و طبل را بازی می کند.‬

Name

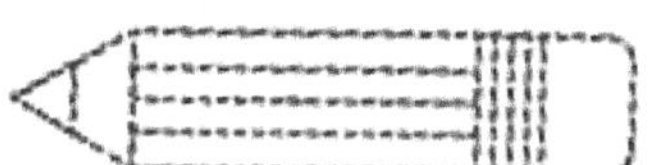

I Can...

- ☐ read the 1st sentence.
- ☐ read the 2nd sentence.
- ☐ make a sentence from a picture.
- ☐ color a picture.
- ☐ Draw a picture.

The dinosaur is a rock star.

.دایناسور یک ستاره راک است

The dragon is playing the guitar.

.اژدها در حال نواختن گیتار است

Name

I Can...

- ☐ read the 1st sentence.
- ☐ read the 2nd sentence.
- ☐ make a sentence from a picture.
- ☐ color a picture.
- ☐ Draw a picture.

The nurse helps the doctor.

پرستار به پزشک کمک می کند

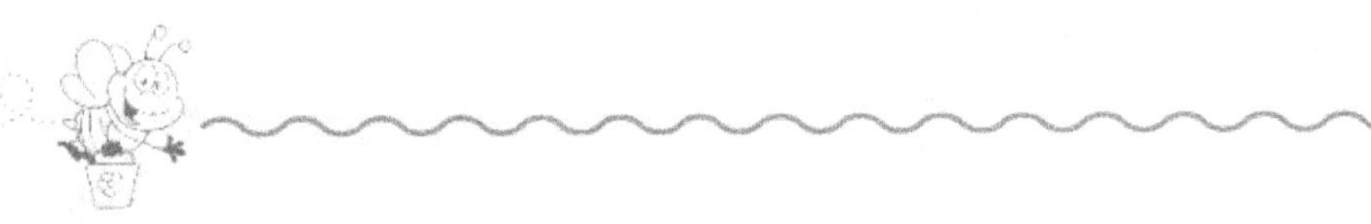

The nurse looks scary, holding a syringe.

پرستار ترسناک به نظر می رسد ، و دارای یک سرنگ است

Name 

44

She is wearing a crown.

.تاج پوشیده است

The queen bee has a beautiful wand.

.زنبور ملکه دارای یک گرز زیبا است

Name

I Can...

- [ ] read the 1st sentence.
- [ ] read the 2nd sentence.
- [ ] make a sentence from a picture.
- [ ] color a picture.
- [ ] Draw a picture.

It is orange and black.

به رنگ نارنجی و سیاه است.

The tiger is wearing a bow on its neck.

ببر بر روی گردن خود کمان پوشیده است.

Name

I Can...

- [ ] read the 1st sentence.
- [ ] read the 2nd sentence.
- [ ] make a sentence from a picture.
- [ ] color a picture.
- [ ] Draw a picture.

The boy is carrying a lot of books.

پسر بچه کتابهای زیادی را حمل می کند

The boy is carrying so many books!

اپسر بچه کتابهای زیادی را حمل می کند

Name

I Can...

- [ ] read the 1st sentence.
- [ ] read the 2nd sentence.
- [ ] make a sentence from a picture.
- [ ] color a picture.
- [ ] Draw a picture.

The pizza looks delicious.

پیتزا خوشمزه به نظر می رسد

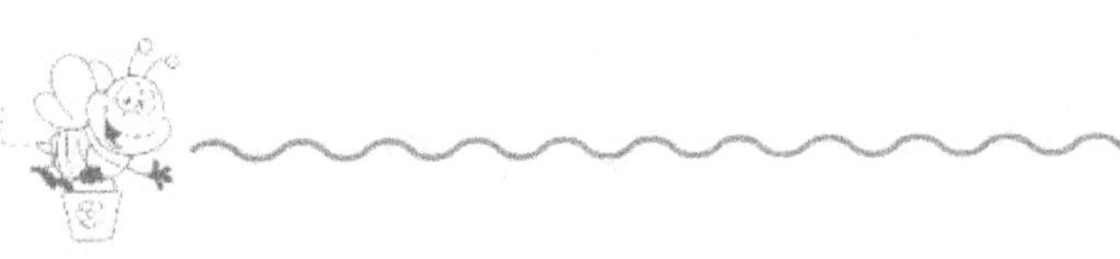

The waiter is serving steaming hot pizza.

پیشخدمت در خدمت بخار پیتزا داغ است

Name

I Can...

- [ ] read the 1st sentence.
- [ ] read the 2nd sentence.
- [ ] make a sentence from a picture.
- [ ] color a picture.
- [ ] Draw a picture.

That is my dad's computer.

این کامپیوتر پدرم است.

My dad works on the computer.

پدر من روی رایانه کار می کند

Name

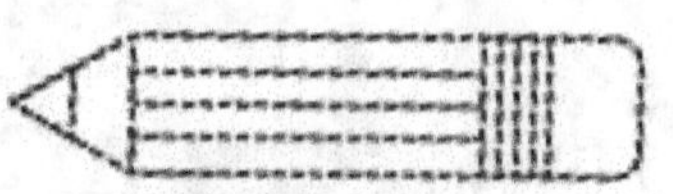

I Can...

- [ ] read the 1st sentence.
- [ ] read the 2nd sentence.
- [ ] make a sentence from a picture.
- [ ] color a picture.
- [ ] Draw a picture.

The farmer has a beard.

کشاورز ریش دارد.

The gardener is going to plant flowers

باغبان قصد دارد گل بکارد

Name

I Can...

- [ ] read the 1st sentence.
- [ ] read the 2nd sentence.
- [ ] make a sentence from a picture.
- [ ] color a picture.
- [ ] Draw a picture.

The strawberry is red.

.توت فرنگی قرمز است

I love to drink strawberry juice.

.من عاشق نوشیدن آب توت فرنگی هستم

Name ____________________ 

I Can...

- [ ] read the 1st sentence.
- [ ] read the 2nd sentence.
- [ ] make a sentence from a picture.
- [ ] color a picture.
- [ ] Draw a picture.

The magician has a wand.

جادوگر یک گرگ دارد.

The wizard likes to work with magic.

جادوگر دوست دارد با جادو کار کند.

52

I Can...

- [ ] read the 1st sentence.
- [ ] read the 2nd sentence.
- [ ] make a sentence from a picture.
- [ ] color a picture.
- [ ] Draw a picture.

Reindeer has a scarf.

.گوزن شمالی روسری دارد

Santa gave reindeer a big present.

.سانتا هدیه بزرگی به گوزن شمالی داد

Name

I Can...

- [ ] read the 1st sentence.
- [ ] read the 2nd sentence.
- [ ] make a sentence from a picture.
- [ ] color a picture.
- [ ] Draw a picture.

I have a lot of pencils.

‫مداد زیادی دارم.‬

I have a lot of brushes and pencils.

‫برس و مداد زیادی دارم.‬

Name

I Can...

- [ ] read the 1st sentence.
- [ ] read the 2nd sentence.
- [ ] make a sentence from a picture.
- [ ] color a picture.
- [ ] Draw a picture.

Santa is fat.

سانتا چاق است.

Santa is having fun.

سانتا در حال تفریح است.

Name

I Can...

- [ ] read the 1st sentence.
- [ ] read the 2nd sentence.
- [ ] make a sentence from a picture.
- [ ] color a picture.
- [ ] Draw a picture.

I have one nose.

من یک بینی دارم

The one is saying its name.

یکی در حال گفتن نام خود است

Name

I Can...

- [ ] read the 1st sentence.
- [ ] read the 2nd sentence.
- [ ] make a sentence from a picture.
- [ ] color a picture.
- [ ] Draw a picture.

I have two ears.

دو گوش دارم.

The number "two" is holding up bunny ears.

شماره "دو" گوشهای بانی را نگه می دارد.

Name

I Can...

- [ ] read the 1st sentence.
- [ ] read the 2nd sentence.
- [ ] make a sentence from a picture.
- [ ] color a picture.
- [ ] Draw a picture.

I have three buttons on my dress.

روی دکمه سه دکمه دارم.

The number "three" is saying you got 3 out of 3.

عدد "سه" می گوید شما 3 از 3 را گرفتید.

Name

I Can...

- [ ] read the 1st sentence.
- [ ] read the 2nd sentence.
- [ ] make a sentence from a picture.
- [ ] color a picture.
- [ ] Draw a picture.

I have 0 tails.

من ٠ دم دارم

The number "zero" is saying, Ok.

.عدد "صفر" در حال گفتن است ، باشه

Name ____________________

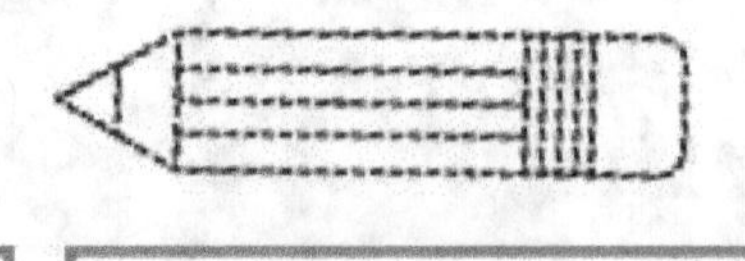

I Can...

- [ ] read the 1st sentence.
- [ ] read the 2nd sentence.
- [ ] make a sentence from a picture.
- [ ] color a picture.
- [ ] Draw a picture.

I have five fingers on 1 of my hands.

پنج انگشت روی 1 دستم دارم.

The number "five" is trying to give you a high five.

عدد "پنج" در تلاش است تا یک پنجم عالی را به شما بدهد.

Name

I Can...

- [ ] read the 1st sentence.
- [ ] read the 2nd sentence.
- [ ] make a sentence from a picture.
- [ ] color a picture.
- [ ] Draw a picture.

My cat has four legs.

گربه من چهار پا دارد.

The number "four" is counting to four.

عدد "چهار" عدد چهار است.

Name

I Can...

- [ ] read the 1st sentence.
- [ ] read the 2nd sentence.
- [ ] make a sentence from a picture.
- [ ] color a picture.
- [ ] Draw a picture.

A butterfly has six legs.

یک پروانه شش پا دارد

The number "six" is saying 1+5=6.

عدد "شش" می گوید 6 = 5 + 1.

Name

I Can...

- [ ] read the 1st sentence.
- [ ] read the 2nd sentence.
- [ ] make a sentence from a picture.
- [ ] color a picture.
- [ ] Draw a picture.

A spider has eight legs.

یک عنکبوت هشت پا دارد

The happy and excited eight is holding up eight fingers

هشت خوشحال و هیجان هشت انگشت در دست دارد

Name ____________________

I Can...

- ☐ read the 1st sentence.
- ☐ read the 2nd sentence.
- ☐ make a sentence from a picture.
- ☐ color a picture.
- ☐ Draw a picture.

The rooster is going to wake people up.

خروس قصد دارد مردم را از خواب بیدار کند.

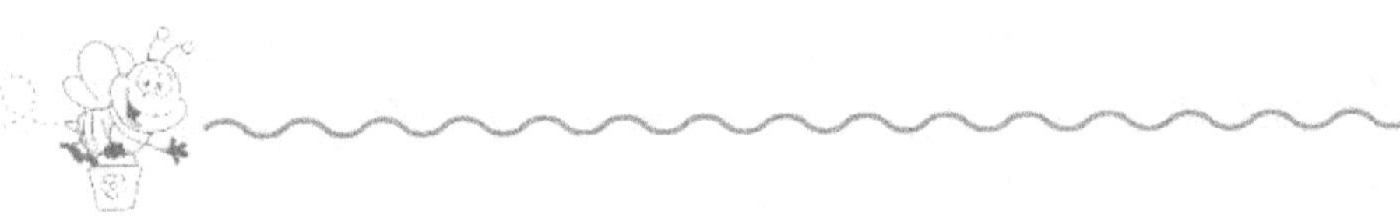

The rooster is on the fence.

خروس روی حصار است.

Name _______________________

I Can...

- [ ] read the 1st sentence.
- [ ] read the 2nd sentence.
- [ ] make a sentence from a picture.
- [ ] color a picture.
- [ ] Draw a picture.

My sister has nine stuffed animals.

.خواهرم نه حیوان پر شده دارد

The smiling number nine is saying its name out loud.

.لبخند شماره نه است که با صدای بلند می گوید

Name

I Can...

- ☐ read the 1st sentence.
- ☐ read the 2nd sentence.
- ☐ make a sentence from a picture.
- ☐ color a picture.
- ☐ Draw a picture.

The baby bee has yellow and black stripes.

زنبور عسل دارای نوارهای زرد و سیاه است.

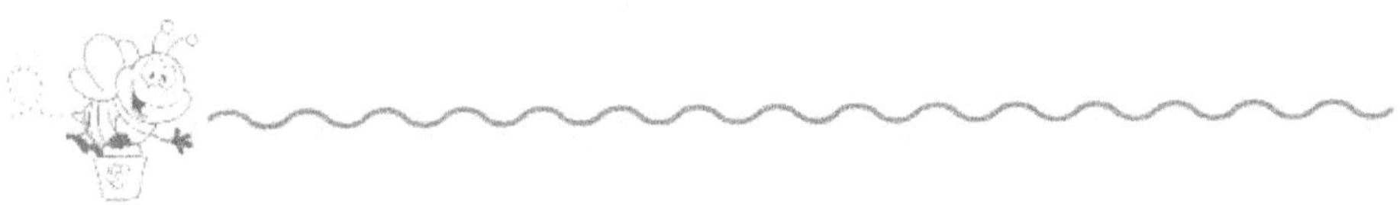

The bee is wearing a pink pacifier to calm itself.

زنبور عسل برای آرام کردن خود از پستانک صورتی استفاده کرده است.

Name _______________

I Can...

- [ ] read the 1st sentence.
- [ ] read the 2nd sentence.
- [ ] make a sentence from a picture.
- [ ] color a picture.
- [ ] Draw a picture.

The ladybug has many spots.

بانوی باگ نقاط زیادی دارد.

The red and black ladybug is just done eating some leaves.

گل سرخ قرمز و سیاه فقط با خوردن بعضی از برگها انجام می شود.

Name

I Can...

- [ ] read the 1st sentence.
- [ ] read the 2nd sentence.
- [ ] make a sentence from a picture.
- [ ] color a picture.
- [ ] Draw a picture.

The sheep are skinny.

گوسفندها لاغر هستند.

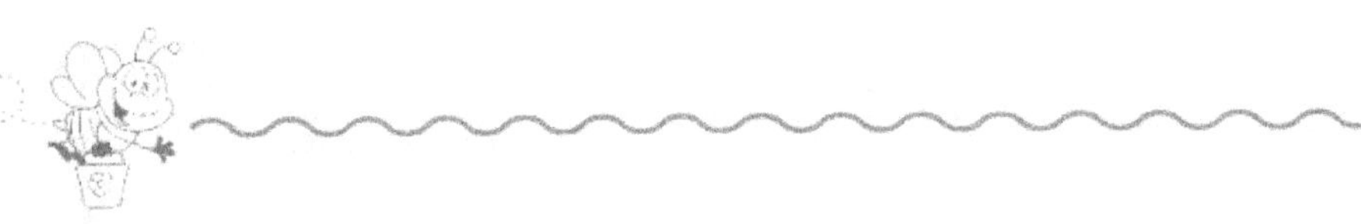

The white sheep have a lot of fluffy white wool to give away.

گوسفند سفید دارای پشم سفید و کرکی زیادی است که می دهد.

Name

I Can...

- [ ] read the 1st sentence.
- [ ] read the 2nd sentence.
- [ ] make a sentence from a picture.
- [ ] color a picture.
- [ ] Draw a picture.

The rabbit is entering an egg painting contest.

خرگوش وارد مسابقه نقاشی تخم مرغ می شود.

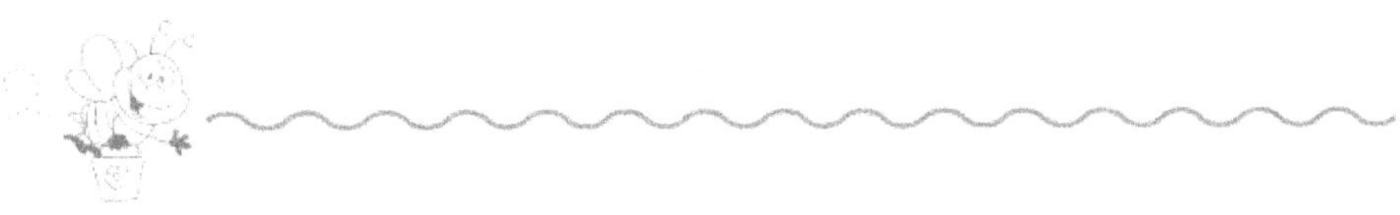

The Easter Bunny is painting a chocolate egg.

عید پاک اسم حیوان دست اموز نقاشی تخم مرغ شکلاتی است.

Name _______________________ 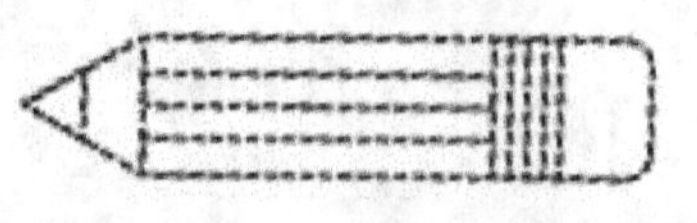

I Can...

- [ ] read the 1st sentence.
- [ ] read the 2nd sentence.
- [ ] make a sentence from a picture.
- [ ] color a picture.
- [ ] Draw a picture.

The owl is a language arts teacher.

.جغد معلم هنر زبان است

An owl is teaching the kids in school about work.

.جغد در حال آموزش به بچه ها در مدرسه در مورد کار است

Name ____________________

I Can...

- [ ] read the 1st sentence.
- [ ] read the 2nd sentence.
- [ ] make a sentence from a picture.
- [ ] color a picture.
- [ ] Draw a picture.

The man has an ancient hammer.

.این مرد چکش باستانی دارد

The builder man has gone to work on a project.

.مرد سازنده برای کار روی یک پروژه رفته است

Name

I Can...

- [ ] read the 1st sentence.
- [ ] read the 2nd sentence.
- [ ] make a sentence from a picture.
- [ ] color a picture.
- [ ] Draw a picture.

The goat has a friend.

بز دوست دارد.

The old goat is proud of its golden bell.

بز قدیمی به زنگ طلایی خود افتخار می کند.

Name

I Can...

- [ ] read the 1st sentence.
- [ ] read the 2nd sentence.
- [ ] make a sentence from a picture.
- [ ] color a picture.
- [ ] Draw a picture.

My mom's friend is a maid.

.دوست مادرم خدمتکار است

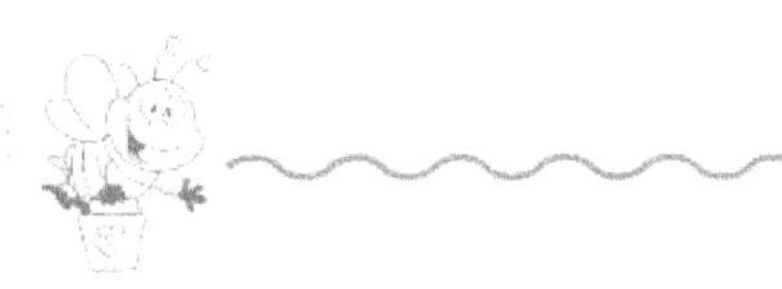

The maid is going to clean the hotel room.

.خدمتکار قصد دارد اتاق هتل را تمیز کند

Name

I Can...

- [ ] read the 1st sentence.
- [ ] read the 2nd sentence.
- [ ] make a sentence from a picture.
- [ ] color a picture.
- [ ] Draw a picture.

I went to the zoo.

به باغ وحش رفتم.

The animals are having a big celebration.

حیوانات در حال برگزاری یک جشن بزرگ هستند.

Name

I Can...

- [ ] read the 1st sentence.
- [ ] read the 2nd sentence.
- [ ] make a sentence from a picture.
- [ ] color a picture.
- [ ] Draw a picture.

The dinosaur has a pillow.

.دایناسور بالشی دارد

The dragon is using the rock to build its house.

.اژدها برای ساخت خانه خود از سنگ استفاده می کند

Name

I Can...

- [ ] read the 1st sentence.
- [ ] read the 2nd sentence.
- [ ] make a sentence from a picture.
- [ ] color a picture.
- [ ] Draw a picture.

The boy is excited to go to school.

پسر از رفتن به مدرسه هیجان زده است

The boy is late for school, so he is sprinting.

پسر برای مدرسه دیر شده است ، بنابراین او در حال چرخش است

Name

I Can...

- read the 1st sentence.
- read the 2nd sentence.
- make a sentence from a picture.
- color a picture.
- Draw a picture.

The kids on the school bus are going to school.

بچه های اتوبوس مدرسه به مدرسه می روند.

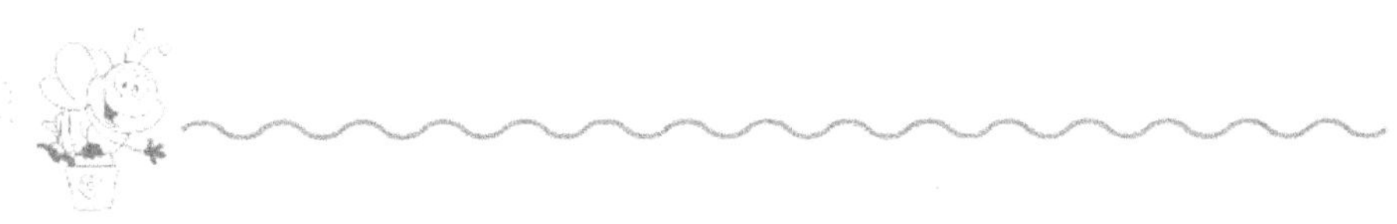

The children are going on a field trip on the yellow bus.

بچه ها با اتوبوس زرد به یک سفر میدانی می روند.

Name

I Can...

- [ ] read the 1st sentence.
- [ ] read the 2nd sentence.
- [ ] make a sentence from a picture.
- [ ] color a picture.
- [ ] Draw a picture.

The cobra is very lovely.

‫کبرا بسیار دوست داشتنی است.‬

The rattlesnake is looking for its dinner.

‫نژاد چوبی به دنبال شام است.‬

I Can...

- [ ] read the 1st sentence.
- [ ] read the 2nd sentence.
- [ ] make a sentence from a picture.
- [ ] color a picture.
- [ ] Draw a picture.

That is a fat dog!

این یک سگ چاق است

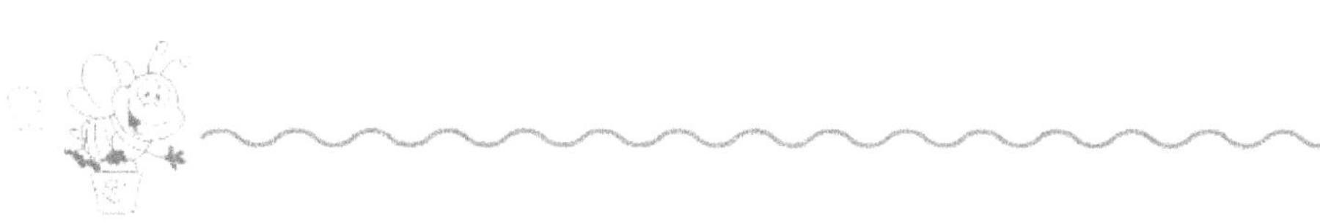

This dog is wagging its tail for more treats.

این سگ برای رفتارهای بیشتر دم خود را تار می کند.

Name 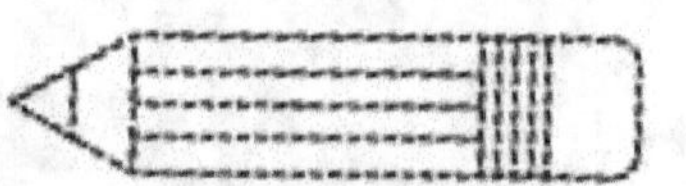

I Can...

- [ ] read the 1st sentence.
- [ ] read the 2nd sentence.
- [ ] make a sentence from a picture.
- [ ] color a picture.
- [ ] Draw a picture.

The elephant lives in the zoo.

فیل در باغ وحش زندگی می کند.

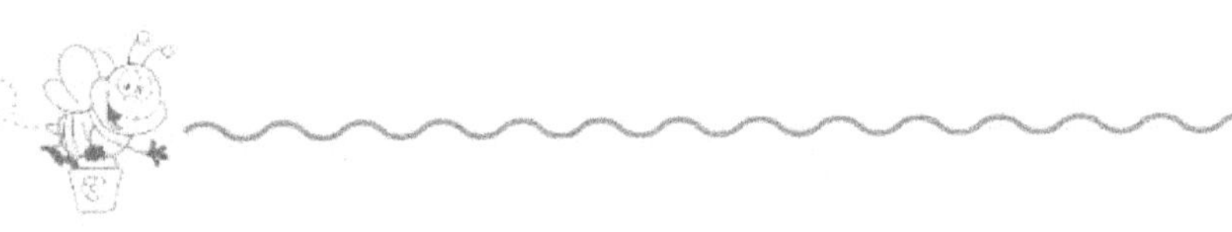

The elephant has a long trunk to spray water.

فیل دارای یک تنه طولانی برای پاشیدن آب است.

Name

I Can...

- [ ] read the 1st sentence.
- [ ] read the 2nd sentence.
- [ ] make a sentence from a picture.
- [ ] color a picture.
- [ ] Draw a picture.

The giraffe eats vegetables.

زرافه سبزیجات می خورد.

The giraffe has an extremely long neck.

زرافه گردنی بسیار طولانی دارد.

Name _______________________

I Can...

- ☐ read the 1st sentence.
- ☐ read the 2nd sentence.
- ☐ make a sentence from a picture.
- ☐ color a picture.
- ☐ Draw a picture.

The chipmunk has a soft tummy.

.چیپونک شکمی نرم دارد

The Chipmunk is about to eat a brown acorn.

.قرار است بلوط قهوه ای بخورد Chipmunk

Name

I Can...

- ☐ read the 1st sentence.
- ☐ read the 2nd sentence.
- ☐ make a sentence from a picture.
- ☐ color a picture.
- ☐ Draw a picture.

I have ten toes in total.

.در کل ده انگشت پا دارم

The one and the zero are holding hands.

.یک و صفر دست در دست دارند

Name

I Can...

- [ ] read the 1st sentence.
- [ ] read the 2nd sentence.
- [ ] make a sentence from a picture.
- [ ] color a picture.
- [ ] Draw a picture.

The alligator is jumping.

تمساح در حال پرش است.

The crocodile is excited.

تمساح هیجان زده است.

Name

I Can...

- [ ] read the 1st sentence.
- [ ] read the 2nd sentence.
- [ ] make a sentence from a picture.
- [ ] color a picture.
- [ ] Draw a picture.

I found an ant.

مورچه پیدا کردم

The ant is telling a story.

.مورچه داستان را می گوید

Name ________________________ 

I Can...

- [ ] read the 1st sentence.
- [ ] read the 2nd sentence.
- [ ] make a sentence from a picture.
- [ ] color a picture.
- [ ] Draw a picture.

The bat sleeps upside down.

خفاش وارونه می خوابد.

The bat is ready to fly.

خفاش آماده پرواز است.

Name

I Can...

- [ ] read the 1st sentence.
- [ ] read the 2nd sentence.
- [ ] make a sentence from a picture.
- [ ] color a picture.
- [ ] Draw a picture.

The cat is very tired.

.گربه بسیار خسته است

The cat is taking a nap.

.گربه در حال چرت زدن است

Name

I Can...

- ☐ read the 1st sentence.
- ☐ read the 2nd sentence.
- ☐ make a sentence from a picture.
- ☐ color a picture.
- ☐ Draw a picture.

The dog likes to play.

سگ دوست دارد بازی کند.

The dog is playing with a bone.

سگ با استخوان بازی می کند.

Name

I Can...

- [ ] read the 1st sentence.
- [ ] read the 2nd sentence.
- [ ] make a sentence from a picture.
- [ ] color a picture.
- [ ] Draw a picture.

The elephant has eyelashes.

فیل مژه دارد.

The elephant is shy.

فیل خجالتی است.

Name

I Can...

- [ ] read the 1st sentence.
- [ ] read the 2nd sentence.
- [ ] make a sentence from a picture.
- [ ] color a picture.
- [ ] Draw a picture.

The frog is hopping.

قورباغه در حال پرت شدن است.

The frog is trying to catch the fly.

قورباغه در حال تلاش برای گرفتن پرواز است.

Name

I Can...

- [ ] read the 1st sentence.
- [ ] read the 2nd sentence.
- [ ] make a sentence from a picture.
- [ ] color a picture.
- [ ] Draw a picture.

The goat is sleepily walking around.

بز در حال گذر از خواب است.

The goat is eating grass.

بز علف می خورد.

Name

I Can...

- [ ] read the 1st sentence.
- [ ] read the 2nd sentence.
- [ ] make a sentence from a picture.
- [ ] color a picture.
- [ ] Draw a picture.

The hippo has a big head.

کرگدن سر بزرگی دارد.

The hippo has a big head.

کرگدن سر بزرگی دارد.

I Can...

- [ ] read the 1st sentence.
- [ ] read the 2nd sentence.
- [ ] make a sentence from a picture.
- [ ] color a picture.
- [ ] Draw a picture.

The iguana has a long tail.

ایگوانا دم بلند دارد.

The iguana is hiding behind the letter I.

ایگوانا در پشت حرف I مخفی شده است.

Name

I Can...

- [ ] read the 1st sentence.
- [ ] read the 2nd sentence.
- [ ] make a sentence from a picture.
- [ ] color a picture.
- [ ] Draw a picture.

Mom bought a new bottle of jam.

.مامان یه بطری مربای جدید خرید

There is jam on the bread.

.مربا روی نان است

Name

I Can...

- [ ] read the 1st sentence.
- [ ] read the 2nd sentence.
- [ ] make a sentence from a picture.
- [ ] color a picture.
- [ ] Draw a picture.

The kite has a beautiful tail.

بادبادک دم زیبایی دارد.

The kite is on the ground.

بادبادک روی زمین است.

Name

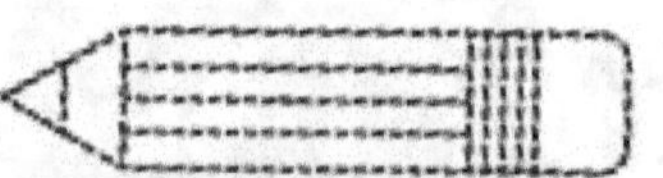

I Can...

- ☐ read the 1st sentence.
- ☐ read the 2nd sentence.
- ☐ make a sentence from a picture.
- ☐ color a picture.
- ☐ Draw a picture.

The lion is timid.

.شیر ترسو است

The lion is big.

.شیر بزرگ است

I Can...

- [ ] read the 1st sentence.
- [ ] read the 2nd sentence.
- [ ] make a sentence from a picture.
- [ ] color a picture.
- [ ] Draw a picture.

I like mice.

من موش ها را دوست دارم

A rat is on top of the letter M

است M موش روی حرف

Name

I Can...

- [ ] read the 1st sentence.
- [ ] read the 2nd sentence.
- [ ] make a sentence from a picture.
- [ ] color a picture.
- [ ] Draw a picture.

The nose is breathing.

بینی نفس می کشد.

The letter N stands for a nose.

حرف N بینی است مخفف.

Name

I Can...

- [ ] read the 1st sentence.
- [ ] read the 2nd sentence.
- [ ] make a sentence from a picture.
- [ ] color a picture.
- [ ] Draw a picture.

The octopus lives underwater.

اختاپوس در زیر آب زندگی می کند.

The octopus has eight tentacles.

هشت پا دارای هشت شاخک است.

Name

I Can...

- [ ] read the 1st sentence.
- [ ] read the 2nd sentence.
- [ ] make a sentence from a picture.
- [ ] color a picture.
- [ ] Draw a picture.

The penguin eats fish.

پنگوئن ماهی می خورد

The penguin lives in the arctic.

پنگوئن در قطب شمال زندگی می کند

Name

I Can...

- [ ] read the 1st sentence.
- [ ] read the 2nd sentence.
- [ ] make a sentence from a picture.
- [ ] color a picture.
- [ ] Draw a picture.

The queen has a wand.

ملکه یک گرگ دارد.

The queen is beautiful.

ملکه زیباست.

Name

I Can...

- ☐ read the 1st sentence.
- ☐ read the 2nd sentence.
- ☐ make a sentence from a picture.
- ☐ color a picture.
- ☐ Draw a picture.

The rabbit has long ears.

.خرگوش گوش های بلند دارد

The rabbit is thinking about something.

.خرگوش به چیزی فکر می کند

I Can...

- [ ] read the 1st sentence.
- [ ] read the 2nd sentence.
- [ ] make a sentence from a picture.
- [ ] color a picture.
- [ ] Draw a picture.

The snake has polka dots.

مار دارای نقاط پولکا است.

The snake is licking its lip because it is hungry.

مار به دلیل گرسنگی ، لب خود را لیس می زند.

Name

I Can...

- [ ] read the 1st sentence.
- [ ] read the 2nd sentence.
- [ ] make a sentence from a picture.
- [ ] color a picture.
- [ ] Draw a picture.

The tortoise has a pointy shell.

لاک پشت پوسته ای برجسته دارد.

The turtle has a robust shell but is very slow.

لاک پشت پوسته محکم دارد اما بسیار کند است.

Name

I Can...

- [ ] read the 1st sentence.
- [ ] read the 2nd sentence.
- [ ] make a sentence from a picture.
- [ ] color a picture.
- [ ] Draw a picture.

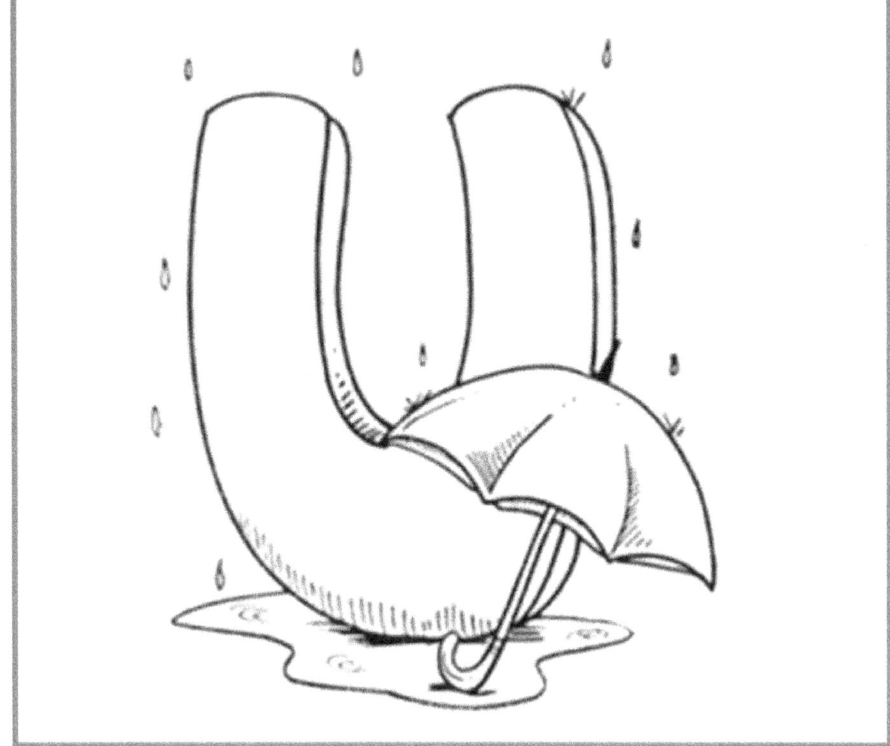

It's raining.

هوا بارانی است.

We use the umbrella when it's raining.

وقتی باران می بارد از چتر استفاده می کنیم.

Name

I Can...

- [ ] read the 1st sentence.
- [ ] read the 2nd sentence.
- [ ] make a sentence from a picture.
- [ ] color a picture.
- [ ] Draw a picture.

The violin is a musical instrument.

.ویولن یک ساز موسیقی است

A violin can play beautiful music if played correctly.

یک ویولن می تواند در صورت پخش صحیح موسیقی زیبا را پخش کند.

Name

I Can...

- [ ] read the 1st sentence.
- [ ] read the 2nd sentence.
- [ ] make a sentence from a picture.
- [ ] color a picture.
- [ ] Draw a picture.

The walrus has a friend.

.گردو یک دوست دارد

The walrus has unusually sharp teeth.

.گردو دندانهای غیر معمول تیزی دارد

Name

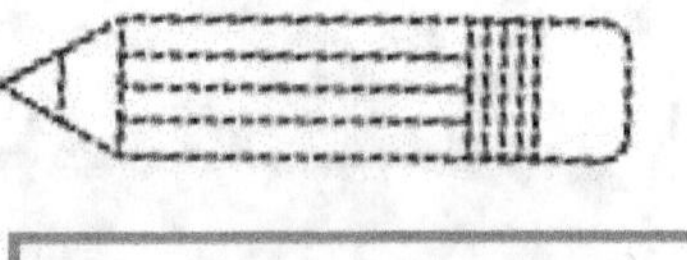

I Can...

- [ ] read the 1st sentence.
- [ ] read the 2nd sentence.
- [ ] make a sentence from a picture.
- [ ] color a picture.
- [ ] Draw a picture.

The xylophone is a colorful instrument.

xylophone ابزاری رنگی است.

The xylophone is an instrument like the piano.

xylophone ابزاری مانند پیانو است.

I Can...

- [ ] read the 1st sentence.
- [ ] read the 2nd sentence.
- [ ] make a sentence from a picture.
- [ ] color a picture.
- [ ] Draw a picture.

The boy has a little hat.

پسر یک کلاه کوچک دارد

The boy is having fun playing with a yoyo.

پسر در حال تفریح با یویو است

Name

I Can...

- [ ] read the 1st sentence.
- [ ] read the 2nd sentence.
- [ ] make a sentence from a picture.
- [ ] color a picture.
- [ ] Draw a picture.

The zebra has a tail.

گورخر دم دارد.

The zebra has black and white stripes.

گورخر دارای نوارهای سیاه و سفید است.

Name

I Can...

- [ ] read the 1st sentence.
- [ ] read the 2nd sentence.
- [ ] make a sentence from a picture.
- [ ] color a picture.
- [ ] Draw a picture.

I have a candle on my cake.

من روی کیک خود شمع دارم.

I had a small birthday cake for my party.

برای مهمانی خود یک کیک تولد کوچک داشتم.

Name

I Can...

- [ ] read the 1st sentence.
- [ ] read the 2nd sentence.
- [ ] make a sentence from a picture.
- [ ] color a picture.
- [ ] Draw a picture.

The astronaut is going on a mission.

فضانورد در حال انجام یک مأموریت است.

An astronaut has to explore our universe so that we would have more knowledge.

یک فضانورد باید جهان خود را کشف کند تا ما دانش بیشتری داشته باشیم.

Name

I Can...

- [ ] read the 1st sentence.
- [ ] read the 2nd sentence.
- [ ] make a sentence from a picture.
- [ ] color a picture.
- [ ] Draw a picture.

The samurai is going for a morning jog.

سامورایی برای یک جوی صبحگاهی می رود.

The samurai is training to become good at fighting.

سامورایی ها در حال آموزش هستند تا در جنگ خوب شوند.

Name 

I Can...

- [ ] read the 1st sentence.
- [ ] read the 2nd sentence.
- [ ] make a sentence from a picture.
- [ ] color a picture.
- [ ] Draw a picture.

My friend is having a gigantic cake.

دوست من در حال تهیه کیک غول پیکر است.

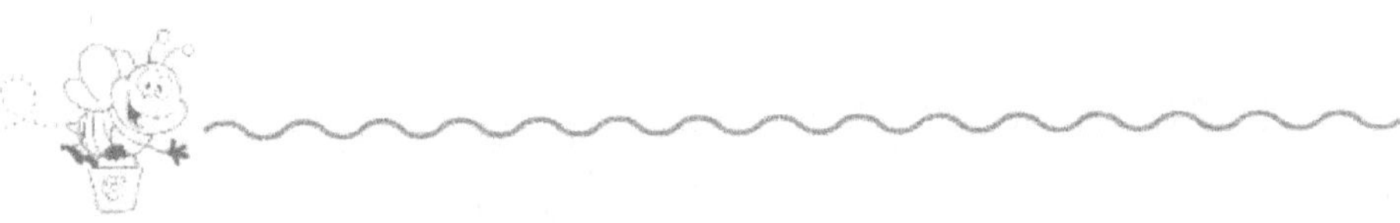

I had a humongous birthday cake for my celebration.

من برای جشن خود یک کیک تولد ناموزون داشتم.

I Can...

- [ ] read the 1st sentence.
- [ ] read the 2nd sentence.
- [ ] make a sentence from a picture.
- [ ] color a picture.
- [ ] Draw a picture.

The frog is chasing the fly.

‫قورباغه پرواز را تعقیب می کند‪.‬

The green frog is trying to catch the fly.

‫قورباغه سبز سعی در پرواز دارد‪.‬

Name

I Can...

- ☐ read the 1st sentence.
- ☐ read the 2nd sentence.
- ☐ make a sentence from a picture.
- ☐ color a picture.
- ☐ Draw a picture.

The ladybug has six legs.

.بانوی بانگ شش پا دارد

The ladybug is on the leaf.

.گل سرخ روی برگ است

Name

I Can...

- [ ] read the 1st sentence.
- [ ] read the 2nd sentence.
- [ ] make a sentence from a picture.
- [ ] color a picture.
- [ ] Draw a picture.

The dragon is sick.

اژدها بیمار است.

The dragon just ate something spicy, so he needed water.

اژدها فقط چیزی ادویه خورد ، بنابراین به آب احتیاج داشت.

Name

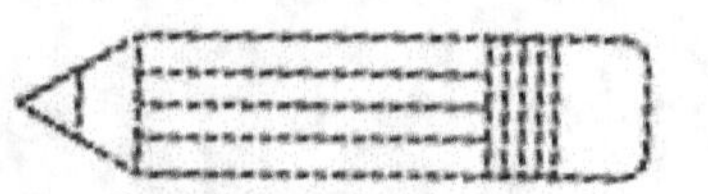

I Can...

- [ ] read the 1st sentence.
- [ ] read the 2nd sentence.
- [ ] make a sentence from a picture.
- [ ] color a picture.
- [ ] Draw a picture.

That is a baby cow.

این یک گاو کودک است.

A little cow is walking around near the barn.

یک گاو کوچک در نزدیکی انبار قدم می زند.

Name

I Can...

- [ ] read the 1st sentence.
- [ ] read the 2nd sentence.
- [ ] make a sentence from a picture.
- [ ] color a picture.
- [ ] Draw a picture.

The frog has a big smile.

.قورباغه لبخند بزرگی دارد

The frog is smiling because it is happy.

.قورباغه لبخند می زند زیرا خوشحال است

Name _______________

I Can...

- [ ] read the 1st sentence.
- [ ] read the 2nd sentence.
- [ ] make a sentence from a picture.
- [ ] color a picture.
- [ ] Draw a picture.

The frog has a big mouth.

قورباغه دهان بزرگی دارد.

The frog is waving to us.

قورباغه به سمت ما موج می زند.

www.ingramcontent.com/pod-product-compliance
Lightning Source LLC
Chambersburg PA
CBHW081344160726
48000CB00010B/3220